THE · BOOK · OF
BABIES

PHOTOGRAPHED BY JO FOORD

RANDOM HOUSE
NEW YORK

This is a Dorling Kindersley Book
published by Random House, Inc.

Senior Editor   Jane Yorke
Assistant Editor   Ann Rosen
Senior Art Editor   Mark Richards
Art Editor   Rowena Alsey
Production   Marguerite Fenn
Photography by   Jo Foord

First American Edition, 1991

Dorling Kindersley would like to thank the
following babies: Elliot Allan, Elliot Baum,
Leila Bennir, Scarlet Bovington, Pascale Cappleton,
Robert Conlan, Hollie Conway, Rachel Earle,
Joshua Green, Neil Gweilo, Joshua Rosen,
Simon Salhotra, Emma Swan, Daniel Thacker,
Daniel Waite, and Elizabeth Wann.

Library of Congress Cataloging-in-Publication Data
Foord, Jo.
    The book of babies : a first picture book of all the things that
babies do : photographs / by Jo Foord. – 1st American ed.
        p.   cm.
    "A Dorling Kindersley Book" – T.p. verso.
    Summary : Photographs of babies in motion demonstrate the variety
of expressions and poses seen in everyday situations.
    ISBN 0-679-80955-4 (trade). – ISBN 0-679-90955-9 (lib. bdg.)
    1. Infants – Juvenile literature.   [1. Babies.]   I. Title.
HQ774. F66   1991
305.23'2'0222–dc20   90-39490 CIP AC

Manufactured in Belgium

10 9 8 7 6 5 4 3

Making Faces
▼
Kicking
▼
Crawling
▼
Busy Hands
▼
Standing
▼
Playing
▼
On the Move
▼
Eating
▼
Dressing
▼
Bathing
▼
Sleeping

Making Faces

Hello baby,

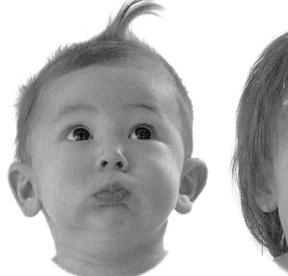

Baby faces of all kinds – which ones can you make?

Funny face, grumpy face – rub a tearful eye –

silly baby, happy baby, sleepy baby.

Sunny face, smiley face, sad, or wide awake?

watchful face, thoughtful face. Baby, please don't cry!

Kicking

Chubby legs that reach and sprawl –

Two strong legs that wave around,

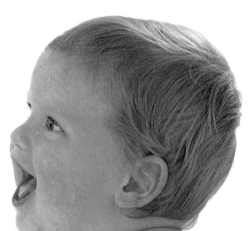

Baby's getting really strong!

cross them over, hold the ball.

push, and stretch out on the ground.

He'll be crawling before long.

Crawling

Baby sets off for a crawl,

Creeping at a steady pace.

On hands and knees, ready . . . set . . . play!

tries to catch the bouncing ball.

These three babies have a race.

Push the choo-choo . . . chug away!

Busy Hands

Tiny hands pat and clap,

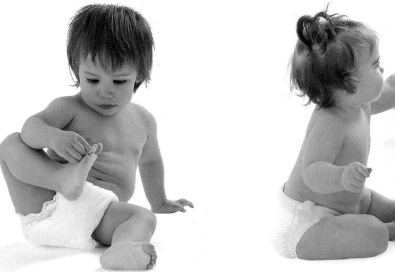

Count ten fingers. Count ten toes. Careful, baby –

Little hands play peekaboo.

touch and point, and poke and tap.

watch that nose!

They also wave bye-bye to you!

Standing

Baby pushes off the ground. Baby stands up tall.

Hands down and bottoms up. Reach out for the cart.

Standing baby, get that ball – steady on those feet.

Baby's looking wobbly. Baby takes a fall!

Look at baby walking now. Baby's made a start!

Dancing baby jumps and rocks, bouncing to the beat.

Playing

Bang the drum! Make a noise!

Toys to push and toys to share.

Blocks to sort – red, green, and blue.

Blocks are baby's favorite toys.

Balls to toss up in the air.

Books are fun to look at too.

On the Move

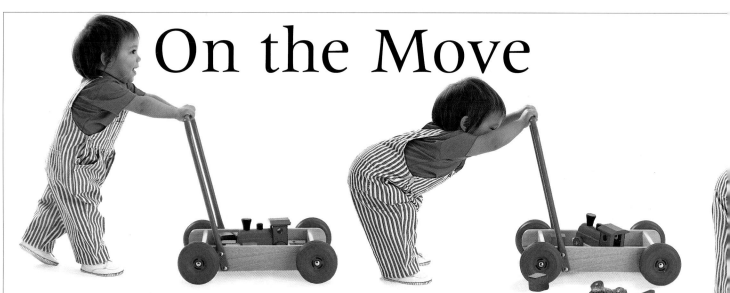

Hold on tight, take it slow. Push the cart along.

Walk and trot, march and run. On two feet, having fun.

Hop aboard, grab the handles. Set out for a ride.

Toys fall out – pick them up. Baby's going strong.

Count the steps – one, two, three. Baby's walking easily.

Push along, spin those wheels. Look at baby glide!

Eating

Nibble a snack on the floor.

Crunchy apples, by the slice.

Tasty juice from a cup.

Bang a spoon; call out for more.

Crispy crackers – aren't they nice?

Milk in a bottle, drink it up!

Dressing

Shirt on, overalls up, baby's wearing blue.

Dress up for a rainy day.

One sock on, pull on two, time to find that other shoe.

Get set, here's a hat . . . don't forget that shoe!

On with the coat, and out to play!

All dressed now, off he races. Someone tie that baby's laces!

Bathing

The water's fine, climb into the tub.

Pop a bubble here and there.

Bathtime's over, take a rest.

Squeeze the sponge, wash, and scrub.

Dry that body, dry that hair.

Sleepy baby, go get dressed.

Sleeping

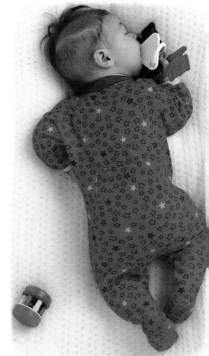

Baby holds a rattle, rolls over, goes to sleep.

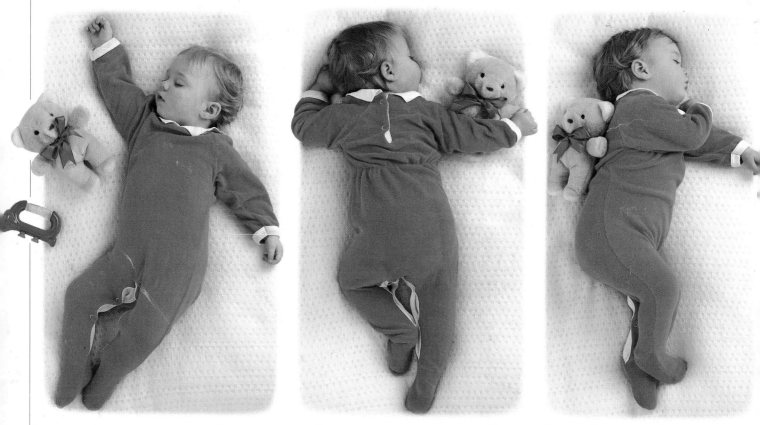

Baby stretches out, eyes closed tight.